Power at Your
FINGERTIPS

Robert Balliet

 www.trafford.com

North America & international
toll-free: 1 888 232 4444 (USA & Canada)
fax: 812 355 4082

Dedication:

I dedicate this book with love and gratitude to my immediate and extended family, especially
my son,
Francis and his wife Carolyn;
and most especially their daughter
and my dear granddaughter Tresia Alise;
my daughter
Elizabeth and her husband Bob,
and most especially their children
and my dear grandchildren:
grandson, Izaak Christopher,
and
granddaughter Syler Macie.

God bless you all!

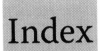

Index

POWER AT YOUR FINGERTIPS

◆ Introduction

How often have you heard the phrase, *"make every vote count,"* during the voting fiascos of the presidential election years of 2000 and, to a lesser degree, 2004? How many times have you learned that in a particularly close local election a candidate or issue was voted or decided upon by just one vote? I cannot overemphasize the importance of one vote in our democratic system of government.

Voting is just one of the enumerated rights of our Federal and State Constitution. I urge you to exercise that right responsibly every time you get the chance.

This book, however, is not about elections, or voting. It is about another right specifically guaranteed by the US Constitution, **the right to petition the government for a "redress of grievance"** (*Amendment 1, Section 1, US Constitution*). Of course, this right to petition can take many forms and, as you will see, is not limited to communicating with the government.

For my purpose here it pertains to verbal and, specifically, <u>written communication</u>. There is indeed **"power at your fingertips"** whether you handwrite, type, or use the ever present computer. (*What did we do before computers? One time, while visiting the local library with my then six-year-old inquisitive granddaughter Syler, she spotted several antique manual typewriters, and wanted to know what those contraptions were – she was fascinated by them.*)

Never underestimate the **power at your fingertips**. Anyone who uses the pen, the typewriter, or the computer, can exercise that power! While petitions (*when petitioning the government*) usually contain more than one name and the amount of influence admitted by those to whom the petition is addressed is many times commensurate with the number of names on the petition, never underestimate the **power at your fingertips**, even when it is used by only one person. **You**!

You, intelligently and professionally communicating with a creditor, a business, a private party, or a governmental agency can often achieve the desired result. Many of my fellow citizens, for one reason or another, choose not to use this powerful tool at their fingertips.

For many years now I have helped people resolve problems, correct a personal injustice, or address a financial difficulty, by working with them to communicate their complaints, making suggestions to resolve those complaints and to follow up or appeal unfavorable decisions that had been made earlier. In most cases, I have found that people are either not aware of how to communicate effectively, or with whom to communicate. They don't have the time – or the knowledge - to find out who in government or in business has oversight responsibility - in other words: Who is that government agent's or business agent's "boss" if any - to influence the decision-making process favorably. That is what I refer to as "third party involvement."

I have heard some friends or family members say: "What's the use?" "Why bother? No one is listening!" "They'll do whatever they want anyway!" or, "I'm just one individual. They don't care what I have to say." Yet, in almost every case where I have helped these people to communicate, sometimes over their initial objections, the outcome was successful. In every such case they were delighted, but they were surprised - they simply did not realize beforehand that: You have **power at your fingertips**!

The purpose of this book, then, is to educate the reader on how he or she, as a consumer or a citizen, can exercise the **power (at their fingertips)**, solve problems with private parties, creditors, businesses, or government agencies, by simply and effectively communicating with them. While I cannot guarantee a successful outcome in a particular case, this book will walk you through the communications process step by step and help you in your attempt to be successful.

In the final analysis, I hope you will appreciate the influence (**power**) you, as an individual, can exert on a particular person, governmental or business entity, in the decision-making process, possibly providing you with benefits, rectifying errors or injustices, or simply giving you a voice or input in their deliberations for yourself, your friends, or your community. And all this for the price of a phone call, an e-mail, or a postage stamp! Good luck in your endeavor!

Bob Balliet, Author

NOTE: I am not an attorney-at-law, and it is important that the reader understands that this book does not in any way take the place of proper legal counsel or action, nor is it attempting to give legal advice. Should your situation, in your judgment, or by law, call for you to consult an attorney, I urge you to do so. *Any written communications produced by you with the help of this book can, nevertheless, be helpful should you meet with a lawyer.*

Communicating with
Private Parties and/or Businesses

THERE MAY COME a time when you have to resolve a problem or an issue with a **private party** or a **business**. By private party I mean your neighbor, a co-worker, or someone not acting in a business or governmental capacity. The **methods of communication** with a private party or a business and the **content of** that **communication**, as well as any **third party involvement and/or follow-up/appeal action** is different from communicating with governmental agencies – that will be discussed in detail in the next chapters.

(A) Private Parties

- ### Methods of Communication.

    Let's say you have a problem or an issue with your neighbor. You can choose to address that problem or discuss that issue by:

    Talking to your neighbor. Regardless of the nature of your relationship with your neighbor, always be respectful or at least civil. Introduce yourself if you don't already know each other, and inform him/her of your concern. Offer a reasonable suggestion, including your part in it, if any, in contributing to the equitable resolution of the problem.

    Example: Your neighbor's dog keeps getting into your yard through a hole in the fence you share. Your attempts to patch up the hole on your side have not been successful. Voice your concern about the safety of your children and the damage his/her dog is causing in your yard. Show him/her the damage. You may want to offer to share in the cost of replacing that portion of the fence. Point out to your neighbor that *your homeowner's insurance - as well as your neighbor's, if he/she has any, - may offset a good portion of that cost.* Listen to your neighbor's response. Thank him/her for listening. If you are in agreement, proceed to implement it according to the agreed upon timetable. If your neighbor's response is negative, non-cooperative, or hostile, it is best not to engage in an argument. Just return to your home.

    If the response was positive: <u>Go home, write down who you talked to, what was discussed and agreed upon and proceed to follow through.</u> *Keep the record of your discussion until the problem is resolved – the fence has been repaired or replaced and the insurance company has settled.*

    If the response was negative, non-cooperative, or hostile: Go home, write down who you talked to, what was discussed, what you offered to help resolve the problem, and your neighbor's response. In this example you have several options, including *writing a letter to your neighbor*, and/or *taking administrative or legal actions*.

Writing a letter to your neighbor.

You have attempted to settle the matter in an informal/verbal way, and, for whatever reason, you did not accomplish your goal. It is time to put things "in writing."

Putting things "in writing" affords you the opportunity to accomplish several things. It helps to:

Create a written record of your attempt to settle a problem;
Organize things in a way that makes future actions, if any, easier; and
Serve as a point of reference for solving future problems.

You can literally use the **power in your pe**n by handwriting, using a typewriter or – my preferred and recommended use – the handy-dandy computer.

◆ Contents of Communication.

Whatever you decide to use to write your letter, make sure you keep these principles of good letter-writing in mind:
- Use a date and an address line.
- In the first paragraph, introduce yourself and indicate that this letter is a follow-up to a previous meeting.
- (Re)introduce the problem and tell how that problem involves the addressee.
- (Re)offer a solution to that problem, your part in the solution, and how that solution would benefit the addressee.
- Offer a reasonable timeline (usually 30 days – unless less time is more appropriate) by which you expect a response from the addressee and state the possible consequences for not responding in time.
- If you suspect that legal action may be taken by you at some point in time, your last paragraph should read: '*This letter has been sent by certified mail to ascertain legal receipt of same.*'
- End the letter with 'Sincerely,' or some other appropriate courtesy. Type your signature block and a way for you to be contacted (i.e. phone number or e-mail address and/or regular address to which mail can be sent).
- Mail your letter as soon as practicable with sufficient postage – regular, or certified – as appropriate. Keep a copy in a Suspense file for further action, if any.

NOTE: *Your letter should be informative, but not lengthy; organized, but not impersonal; respectful in content and language, but not timid. And, please, make use of "spell-check" or a dictionary!*

HELP: Please see Sample Letters to Private Party

Sample #1 – Letter to Private Party

(City), (Date)

Mr. (&) (Mrs.) (Ms.) (Name of individual)
(Street address), (Apt. or Ste. #)
(City), (State) (Zip code)

Dear Mr. (&) (Mrs.) (Ms.):

This letter is a follow-up to our meeting in person on (date of meeting).

At that first meeting, we discussed the problem your dog is causing by entering my back yard via a hole in our mutual fence. I showed you the damage I believe was done to my property and I voiced concern of the potential injury your dog may cause members of my family, while they are attempting to enjoy the outdoors.

I requested that the fence be repaired and offered to help you with the cost of the material – after any homeowner's insurance settlement. Your response, while cordial, was unsatisfactory. Your words, as I recall them were: 'I have more important things to do than be concerned about a hole in the fence.'

I respectfully request that your reconsider and agree to have the fence repaired within 30 days of receipt of this letter. If, after the aforementioned 30 days, this problem is not resolved to my satisfaction, I reserve the right to take unilateral action to repair the fence and to pursue administrative or legal action to recover your part of the cost, plus any related cost that I incur.

This letter has been sent by certified mail, to ascertain legal receipt of same.

Sincerely,

(Name)
(Street address), (Apt. or Ste. #)
(City), (State) (Zip code)
(Phone number) – not required

Sample #2 – Letter to Private Party

(City), (Date)

Mr. (&) (Mrs.) (Ms.) (Name of individual)
(Street address), (Apt. or Ste. #)
(City), (State) (Zip code)

Dear Mr. (&) (Mrs.) (Ms.)

This letter is a follow-up to our meeting in person on (date of meeting).

At that first meeting, we discussed the problem your continuous and loud music is causing me and my family, as we attempt to enjoy living in our home.

I requested that you be considerate of our (and the rest of your neighbors') need and right to live in peace and tranquility, and for you to consider turning down the volume considerably during the day and completely after 9:00 p.m.

Your response to my request was unsatisfactory and required me to call our local police department – even that police action resolved little.

Accordingly, please be advised that I will consider administrative and/or legal action should you fail to comply immediately with the law as it relates to excessive noise levels and the associated time constraints. You will be responsible for any administrative and/or legal costs resulting from any such action.

This letter has been sent by certified mail to ascertain legal receipt of same.

Sincerely,

(Name)
(Street address), (Apt. or Ste. #)
(City), (State) (Zip code)
(Phone number) – not required

Sample Letter #3 – Letter to Private Party

(City), (Date)

Mr. (&) (Mrs.) (Ms.) (Name of individual)
(Street address), (Apt or Sp #)
(City), (State) (Zip code)

Dear Mr. (&) (Mrs.) (Ms.):

This letter is a follow-up to our meeting in person on (date of meeting).

At that first meeting, we discussed that you failed to pay back the $200.00 you borrowed from me on (date) Please see attached copy of Agreement to Pay Debt.

Your response to my request was unsatisfactory, even hostile, to the point where I felt uncomfortable and returned home.

I respectfully request that you honor your promise to pay your debt no later than 30 days from receipt of this letter. Failure to do so will result in administrative and/or legal action in a court of law. You will then be also responsible for any administrative and/or legal costs resulting from any such action.

This letter has been sent by certified mail to ascertain legal receipt of same.

Sincerely,

(Name)
(Street address), (Apt. or Ste. #)
(City), (State) (Zip code)
(Phone number) – not required

♦ Third Party Involvement.
Taking Administrative or Legal Action.

Okay, time has passed and your neighbor did not respond to your letter, or the response was unsatisfactory. If in your letter, you advised your neighbor that administrative or legal action may, or would follow, now is the time to get a third party involved to help you resolve your problem.

If you choose to take **administrative action**, gather your written records, copies of any letters you sent and verification of receipt of the certified letters (if any) and sit down and prepare another letter.

You must first determine who to escalate this matter to. There appears to be a governmental agency that has oversight responsibility for just about anything that one encounters in life. But, how to find out who that might be? You have several options:

> -your local phone book (White Pages – government section – city, county, state, or federal. *I recommend you stay as "local" as possible.* Try to identify the responsible entity by subject matter [in this example, Animal Control may be appropriate]. Check Appendix A & B)
> - your friends and other neighbors that may have had similar experiences and can help direct you
> - your local government official or representatives
> - your local police department
> - your attorney.

Once you have identified the "responsible" administrative entity it may save you time to call them first and verify that they do, in fact, have oversight jurisdiction.

If there is more than one responsible entity, write down their mailing address for possible later use.

Now you're ready to take administrative follow-up action by writing another letter.

> - Use a date and an address line.
> - In the first paragraph, introduce yourself and the purpose of this letter (i.e. to seek their help in resolving a problem).
> -Introduce the problem by way of a short synopsis and tell how that problem involves your neighbor (*use your original letter to help you*).
> -Indicate what actions you took to resolve this problem and what the response was. Include a copy of your original, follow-up letter(s) and any response you received and refer to them at this time.
> - Request the entity to take appropriate action to resolve this problem.
> -Indicate what action you intend to take should the problem not be resolved in a reasonable time frame.
> -If you suspect that legal action may be taken by you at some point in time, your last paragraph should read: *'This letter has been sent by certified mail to ascertain legal receipt of same.'*
> -End the letter with 'Sincerely,' or some other appropriate courtesy, type your signature block and your contact information (phone number or e-mail address and/or regular address to which mail can be sent).
> - Mail your letter as soon as practicable with sufficient postage – regular, or certified – as appropriate.
> -Keep a copy of this letter, together with all related correspondence in a Suspense file for further action, if any.

NOTE: *Your letter should be informative, but not lengthy; organized, but not impersonal; respectful in content and language, but not timid. And, please, make use of "spell-check" or a dictionary!*

HELP: Please see Sample Letters of Administrative Action to Private Party

Sample Letter #1 – Letter of Administrative Action to Private Party

(City), (Date)

Mr. (&) (Mrs.) (Ms.) (Name of individual)
(Street address), (Apt. or Ste. #)
(City), (State) (Zip code)

Dear Mr. (&) (Mrs.) (Ms.):

The purpose of this letter is to advise you of the following administrative action I have taken as it relates to the unresolved problem of our mutual fence, and as a follow-up to my earlier letter to you, dated --- (copy attached).

I have taken the liberty of contacting my homeowners' insurance company and filed a claim with them to have the damage on our mutual fence repaired. The cost of repair will be $450.00 (equipment and labor). The fence will be repaired on (date). Your portion of the above quoted cost will be $225.00.

You may pay that amount directly to the repairman (or his company) after the fence has been repaired, or you may reimburse me for that amount, if you choose to do it that way. In any case, if you choose not to pay the repairman (or his company) directly, please reimburse me no later than 30 days from the date of the repair. I'll be glad to provide you with a receipt.

I reserve the right to take legal action in a court of law, should payment not be made. You will then be also responsible for any court costs or other legitimate charges resulting from any such action.

This letter has been sent by certified mail to ascertain legal receipt of same.

Sincerely,

(Name)
(Street address), (Apt. or Ste. #)
(City), (State) (Zip code)
(Phone number) – not required

Enclosure
as

Sample Letter #2 – Letter of Administrative Action to Private Party

(City), (Date)

Mr. (&) (Mrs.) (Ms.) (Name of individual)
(Street address), (Apt. or Ste. #)
(City), (State) (Zip code)

Dear Mr. (&) (Mrs.) (Ms.):

The purpose of this letter is to advise you of the following administrative action I have taken as it relates to the unresolved problem of your playing excessive and loud music at all hours of the day and night, and as a follow-up to my earlier letter to you, dated (copy attached).

I have taken the liberty of contacting our homeowners' association and asked them to take appropriate action to restore reasonable peace and tranquility – in accordance with their policy and applicable ordinances, statutes, and/or laws.

I reserve the right to take further legal action in a court of law, should that not resolve the problem quickly enough. You will then be also responsible for any court costs, attorney's fees, or other legitimate charges resulting from any such action.

This letter has been sent by certified mail to ascertain legal receipt of same.

Sincerely,

(Name)
(Street address), (Apt. or Ste. #)
(City), (State) (Zip code)
(Phone number) – not required

Enclosure
  as

Sample Letter #3 – Letter of Administrative Action to Private Party

(City), (Date)

Mr. (&) (Mrs.) (Ms.) (Name of individual)
(Street address), (Apt. or Ste. #)
(City), (State) (Zip code)

Dear Mr. (&) (Mrs.) (Ms.)

The purpose of this letter is to advise you of the action I am considering as it relates to the unresolved problem of your failure to repay me the $200.00 you owe me, and as a follow-up to my earlier letter to you, dated ---- (copy attached).

Pursuant to that letter, I am prepared to take legal action in Small Claims Court to recoup the money you borrowed and promised, but failed to pay as of today. I will proceed with legal action if I have not received full payment by (date).

This letter has been sent by certified mail to ascertain legal receipt of same.

Sincerely,

(Name)
(Street address), (Apt. or Ste. #)
(City), (State) (Zip code)
(Phone number) – not required

Enclosure
 as

If you chose to take **legal action**, gather all your notes and correspondence and **contact your attorney for further action.** *Your copies of the notes and correspondence should help the attorney and you focus on what action to take – so take them with you when you go to your initial appointment.*

If you chose to take the **Small Claims Cour**t route – *to recoup the cost of the repairs you had to make* - without the advice of an attorney, gather all your notes and correspondence, go to your local Small Claims Court and proceed to file a claim. *Your copies of the notes and correspondence should help you fill out your claim – so take them with you when you file your claim.*

Don't forget to include in the amount of compensation you desire: court costs (including amount to have papers served), if any, lost wages or vacation time, if any, and any other legitimate cost you incur as a result of this suit, as appropriate.

Follow any court instructions or lawyer advice you receive.

Make a note of the court date when you receive it and be there on time (with all pertinent documents) ready to present your case.

Once the proceedings are completed and the judge has ruled on your case, follow his/her instructions and keep all pertinent documents until final resolution and at least six months thereafter, unless otherwise instructed by the court.

HELP: Please see Sample Letters of Legal Action to Private Party

Sample #1 - Letter of Legal Action to Private Party (Page 19)
Sample #2 - Letter of Legal Action to Private Party (Page 20)
Sample #3 - Letter of Legal Action to Private Party (Page 21)

Sample Letter #1 – Letter of Legal Action to Private Party

(City), (Date)

Mr. (&) (Mrs.) (Ms.) (Name of individual)
(Street address), (Apt. or Ste. #)
(City), (State) (Zip code)

Dear Mr. (&) (Mrs.) (Ms.):

The purpose of this letter is to advise you of the following legal action I have taken as it relates to your failure to re-imburse me for the cost of repairing our mutual fence, and as a follow-up to my earlier letter to you, dated ---(copy attached).

I have taken the liberty of filing a Small Claims Court action in an effort to compel you to pay your part ($225.00 plus court costs) of the cost of repairing our mutual fence. You will receive appropriate notification to appear from the court.

You can avoid going to court by paying the $225.00 (plus filing fee) to me directly prior to the court appearance date.

This letter has been sent by certified mail to ascertain legal receipt of same.

Sincerely,

(Name)
(Street address), (Apt. or Ste. #)
(City), (State) (Zip code)
(Phone number) – not required

Enclosure
  as

Sample Letter #2 – Letter of Legal Action to Private Party

(City), (Date)

Mr. (&) (Mrs.) (Ms.) (Name of individual)
(Street address), (Apt. or Ste. #)
(City), (State) (Zip code)

Dear Mr. (&) (Mrs.) (Ms.)

The purpose of this letter is to advise you of the following legal action I have taken as it relates to your continued refusal to turn down the volume on your stereo system, your failure to comply with the ruling of the applicable homeowners' association, and as a follow-up to my earlier letter to you, dated --- (copy attached).

I have consulted with the district attorney's office and that office will notify you of any further action they choose to take.

You can reverse this action, by complying with the aforementioned request to turn down the volume forthwith.

Sincerely,

(Name)
(Street address), (Apt. or Ste. #)
(City), (State) (Zip code)
(Phone number) – not required

Enclosure
  as

Sample Letter #3 – Letter of Legal Action to Private Party

(City), (Date)

Mr. (&) (Mrs.) (Ms.) (Name of individual)
(Street address), (Apt. or Ste. #)
(City), (State) (Zip code)

Dear Mr. (&) (Mrs.) (Ms.):

The purpose of this letter is to advise you of the following legal action I have taken as it relates to your failure to pay me the $200.00 (plus court costs), and as a follow-up to my earlier letter to you, dated --- (copy attached).

I have filed an action against you in Small Claims Court in an effort to compel you to pay me the above-mentioned amount. The court will notify you of the court date.

You can avoid this action by paying me directly $200.00 plus the filing fee, prior to the hearing date.

Sincerely,

(Name)
(Street address), (Apt. or Ste. #)
(City), (State) (Zip code)
(Phone number) – not required

Enclosure
   as

• Follow-up/Appeal Actions.

Should your request for action be denied by a third party, the written denial almost always includes instructions on how to appeal. Follow the instructions to the letter. If you have any questions, be sure to call the entity whose decision you are appealing. Then proceed as instructed.

Should the denial of your request either not provide for an appeal, or not address appeals, find out what the next supervisory level of the entity that denied your appeal is. *If you don't know, call them and find out – including name of the office supervisor, phone number, and mailing address.*

Now you're ready to write a letter to take follow-up and/or appeals action!

Fill out any Appeals Form that may be required and attach your letter if permitted – if the appeals instructions don't say, call the entity you are appealing to and ask if it's okay for you to attach your letter.

   - Use a date and an address line.
   - In the first paragraph, introduce yourself and the purpose of this letter (i.e. to seek their help in appealing a written denial).
   - Introduce the problem by way of a short synopsis and explain how that problem involves your neighbor.
   - Indicate what actions you took to resolve this problem and what the response was. Include a copy of your original, follow-up letter(s), and any response you received and refer to them at this time.
   - Request the entity to take appropriate action to reverse the original decision.
   - Indicate what action you intend to take should the problem not be resolved in a reasonable time.

If you suspect that legal action may be taken by you at some point in time, your last paragraph should read: *'This letter has been sent by certified mail to ascertain legal receipt of same'.*

   - End the letter with 'Sincerely,' or some other appropriate courtesy, type your signature block and a way for you to be contacted (i.e. phone number or e-mail address and/or regular address to which mail can be sent).
   - Make sure you list any enclosures below your signature block.
   - Send a copy of this appeal to the entity whose denial you are appealing.
   - Mail your letter as soon as practicable with sufficient postage – regular, or certified – as appropriate.

Keep a copy of this letter, together with all related correspondence in a Suspense file for further action, if any.

NOTE: *Your letter should be informative, but not lengthy; organized, but not impersonal; respectful in content and language, but not timid. And, please, make use of "spell-check" or a dictionary!*

HELP: Please see Sample Letters of Follow-up &/or Appeal to Private Party

Sample Letter #1 – Letter of Follow-up to Private Party

(City), (Date)

Mr. (&) (Mrs.) (Ms.) (Name of individual)
(Street address), (Apt. or Ste. #)
(City), (State) (Zip code)

Dear Mr. (&) (Mrs.) (Ms.):

The purpose of this letter is to advise you that the matter of the repair to our mutual fence and your (payment or reimbursement) of the $225.00 (plus other costs) has been satisfactorily resolved.

The matter is now settled.

Sincerely,

(Name)
(Street address), (Apt. or Ste. #)
(City), (State) (Zip code)
(Phone number) – not required

Enclosure (*List # of enclosures – items you attached, if any*)

Sample Letter #2 – Letter of Follow up to Private Party

(City), (Date)

Mr. (&) (Mrs.) (Ms.) (Name of individual)
(Street address), (Apt. or Ste. #)
(City), (State) (Zip code)

Dear Mr. (&) (Mrs.) (Ms.):

The purpose of this letter is to advise you that the matter of excessive noise emanating from your residence has been satisfactorily resolved.

Thank you for your cooperation.

The matter is now settled.

Sincerely,

(Name)
(Street address), (Apt. or Ste. #)
(City), (State) (Zip code)
(Phone number) – not required

Enclosures (*List # of enclosures – items you attached, if any*)

Sample Letter #3 – Letter of Follow up to Private Party

(City), (Date)

Mr. (&) (Mrs.) (Ms.) (Name of individual)
(Street address), (Apt. or Ste. #)
(City), (State) (Zip code)

Dear Mr. (&) (Mrs.) (Ms.):

The purpose of this letter is to advise you that the matter your payment of $200.00 owed me has been satisfactorily resolved.

I received your (check, money order, and cash) on (date), and I thank you for that payment.

The matter is now settled.

Sincerely,

(Name)
(Street address), (Apt. or Ste. #)
(City), (State) (Zip code)
(Phone number) – not required

Enclosures (*List # of enclosures – items you attached, if any*)

Sample Letter 1 – Letter of Appeal from Private Party

(City), (Date)

Agency (To whom you are appealing)
(Street address), (Ste. or Room # - if any)
(City), (State) (Zip code)

Re: (Case #) – (your LAST NAME, First Name, MI)

Dear (Person who made decision you are appealing, or person to whom you are appealing):

The purpose of this letter is to appeal your decision in the above-referenced case. The reason(s) I am appealing this decision is (are) as follows:

- ✓ State why you are appealing.
- ✓ State change in situation since case began, if any.
- ✓ The Appeals Form you provided has been filled out as requested and this letter is to be made a part of it.

I respectfully request that you reconsider your earlier decision in light of the above-stated reason(s), and invite you to contact me should you have any questions or concerns.

Sincerely,

(Name)
(Street address), (Apt. or Ste. #)
(City), (State) (Zip code)
(Phone number) – not required

Enclosures (Indicate number of enclosures, if any)

Sample Letter 2 – Letter of Appeal from Private Party

(City), (Date)

Agency (To whom you are appealing)
(Street address), (Ste. or Room # - if any)
(City), (State) (Zip code)

Re: (Case #) – (your LAST NAME, First Name, MI)

Dear (Person who made decision you are appealing or person to whom you are appealing).

The purpose of this letter is to advise you that I have decided to appeal your decision in this case. This will be done consistent with the appeals process and within the time prescribed.

Should you have any questions or concerns, please feel free to contact me.

Sincerely,

(Name)
(Street address), (Apt. or Ste. #)
(City), (State) (Zip code)
(Phone number) – Not required

Enclosures (Indicate number of enclosures, if any)

Sample Letter 3 – Letter of Appeal from Private Party

(City), (Date)

Agency (To whom you are appealing)
(Street address), (Ste. or Room # - if any)
(City), (State) (Zip code)

Re: (Case #) – (your LAST NAME, First Name, MI)

Dear (Person who made decision you are appealing, or person to whom you are appealing):

The purpose of this letter is to advise you that the Appeals documents provided by your office, for an appeal in the subject matter case, are attached.

Should you have any questions or concerns, please feel free to contact me.

Sincerely,

(Name)
(Street address), (Apt. or Ste. #)
(City), (State) (Zip code)
(Phone number) – not required

Enclosures (Indicate number of enclosures, if any)

(B) Businesses:

◆ Methods of Communication.

Let's say you have a problem or an issue with a business. You can choose to address that problem or discuss that issue by:

Talking to the proprietor/representative of the business. Regardless of the nature of your relationship with the proprietor/representative of the business, always be respectful or at least civil. Introduce yourself, if you don't already know each other, and inform him/her of your concern. Offer a reasonable solution, including your part, if any, in contributing to the resolution of that problem.

Example: You recently purchased a major item (washing machine, dryer, and/or contract work) and the item purchased, or work performed, is defective. You've decided to contact that business either by phone or in person. *Before you make the contact, locate the applicable warranty documents that you -hopefully - will find among your Important papers.* Introduce yourself, give a brief history of the item purchased or the contract work done, and the defect you have noticed. Also inform the person you are talking to of the warranty you have and ask for instructions to correct the defect, consistent with the warranty (if any). Listen to the business response. Thank him/her for listening. If you are in agreement, proceed to implement it according to the agreed upon instructions/timetable. If the business' response is negative, non-cooperative, or hostile, it is best not to engage in an argument. Just return to your home, or, if on the phone, say goodbye and hang up.

If the response was positive: Go home, write down with whom you talked, what was discussed and agreed upon, and proceed to follow through. Keep this record of your discussion until the problem is resolved, the defect has been repaired, or the item replaced, the warranty was honored and/or the insurance company has settled, as applicable.

If the response was negative, non-cooperative, or hostile: Go home, write down whom you talked to, what was discussed, what you offered to help resolve the problem and business' response. In this example you have several options, including *writing a letter to the business (to make it official)*, and/or *taking administrative or legal action.*

Writing a Letter to a Business.

You have attempted to settle the matter in an informal (verbal) way, and, for whatever reason, you did not accomplish your goal. It is time to put things "in writing."

When you "put things in writing," it affords you the opportunity to accomplish several things:

- Create a written record of your attempts to settle a problem
- Organize things in a way that makes future actions, if any, easier
- Serve as a point of reference for solving future problems.

You can literally use the **power in your pe**n by the use of handwriting, a typewriter, or – my preferred and recommended use – the handy-dandy computer.

◆ Contents of Communication

Whatever you decide to use to write your letter, make sure you keep these principles of good letter-writing in mind:

- Use a date and an address line.
- Below the address line, indicate the account number that you are referring to and the last name, first name and middle initial on the account.
- In the first paragraph introduce yourself and indicate that this letter is a follow-up to a previous meeting, giving a brief history of that encounter.
- (Re)introduce the problem and tell how that problem involves the addressee.
- (Re)offer a solution to that problem, your part in the solution, and how that solution would benefit the addressee, including any applicable warranties.
- Offer a reasonable timeline (usually 30 days – unless less time is more appropriate) by which you expect a response from the addressee and the possible consequences for not responding in time.
- If you suspect that legal action may be taken by you at some point in time, your last paragraph should read: *'This letter has been sent by certified mail to ascertain legal receipt of same.'*
- Make sure you list any enclosures you referred to in your letter.
- End the letter with 'Sincerely,' or some other appropriate courtesy. Type your signature block and a way for you to be contacted (i.e. phone number or e-mail address and/or regular address to which mail can be sent).
- Mail your letter as soon as practicable with sufficient postage – regular, or certified – as appropriate. Keep a copy in a Suspense file for further action, if any.

NOTE: **Your letter should be informative, but not lengthy; organized, but not impersonal; respectful in content and language, but not timid. And, please, make use of "spell-check" or a dictionary!**

HELP: **Please see Sample Letters**

Sample Letter to Creditor

(City), (Date)

(Name of creditor)
(Street or P.O. address of creditor)
(City), (State) (Zip code)

Re: Account # - (Last Name, First Name, Middle Initial of person on account)

Dear (Title or name of contact person – or, if not known, To Whom It May Concern):

The purpose of this letter is to follow up on our (phone) conversation of (date) and satisfactorily resolve any outstanding issues regarding my recently activated and above-referenced credit card.

The problem(s) and/or outstanding issue(s) with my newly acquired card is (are) as follows:

(Explain the problem[s] in a few sentences).

Please take the necessary action to correct the problem(s) outlined above and let me know, within a reasonable time frame, what action(s) you have decided to take.

Sincerely,

(FIRST NAME MI LAST NAME)
(Street address)
(City), (State) (Zip code)
(Phone # - where you can be contacted) - not required.

Sample Letter to Insurance Co.

(City), (Date)

(Name of insurance co.)
(Street or P.O. address of insurance co.)
(City), (State) (Zip code)

Re: Policy # - (Last Name, First Name, Middle Initial of person on policy)

Dear (Title or name of contact person – or, if not known, To Whom It May Concern):

The purpose of this letter is to follow up on our (phone) conversation of (date) and satisfactorily resolve any outstanding issues regarding my above-referenced insurance policy.

The problem(s) and/or outstanding issue(s) with my policy is (are) as follows:

(Explain the problem[s] in a few sentences).

Please take the necessary action to correct the problem(s) outlined above and let me know, within a reasonable time frame, what action(s) you have decided to take.

Sincerely,

(FIRST NAME MI LAST NAME)
(Street address)
(City), (State) (Zip code)
(Phone # - where you can be contacted) - not required.

Sample Letter to Health Care Provider

(City), (Date)

(Name of health care provider)
(Street or P.O. address of insurance co.)
(City), (State) (Zip code)

Re: Account # - (Last Name, First Name, Middle Initial of person on account)

Dear (Title or name of contact person – or, if not known, To Whom It May Concern):

The purpose of this letter is to follow up on our (phone) conversation of (date) and satisfactorily resolve any outstanding issues regarding my above-referenced account.

The problem(s) and/or outstanding issue(s) with my policy is (are) as follows: (Explain the problem[s] in a few sentences).

(Explain the type of corrective action that should be taken and the reason for it [them] in a few sentences).

Please take the necessary action to correct the problem(s) outlined above and let me know, within a reasonable time frame, what action(s) you have decided to take.

Sincerely,

(FIRST NAME MI LAST NAME)
(Street address)
(City), (State) (Zip code)
(Phone # - where you can be contacted) - not required.

Sample Letter to Landlord

(City), (Date)

(Name of landlord)
(Street or P.O. address of landlord)
(City), (State) (Zip code)

Re: (Address & unit number) - (Last Name, First Name, Middle Initial of person on account)

Dear (Title or name of contact person – or, if not known, To Whom It May Concern):

The purpose of this letter is to follow up on our (phone) conversation of (date) and satisfactorily resolve any outstanding issue(s) regarding my (leased/rented) residence.

The problem(s) and/or outstanding issue(s) is (are) as follows:

✓ (List a problem)
✓ (List a problem)

(Explain the type of corrective action that should be taken and the reason for it [them] in a few sentences).

Please take the necessary action to correct the problem(s) outlined above and let me know, within a reasonable time frame, what action(s) you have decided to take.

Sincerely,

(FIRST NAME MI LAST NAME)
(Street address)
(City), (State) (Zip code)
(Phone # - where you can be contacted) - not required

Sample Letter to Collection Agency

(City), (Date)
(Name of collection agency)
(Street or P.O. address of collection agency)
(City), (State) (Zip code)

Re: (Account number) - (Last Name, First Name, Middle Initial of person on collection account)

Dear (Title or name of contact person – or, if not known, To Whom It May Concern):

The purpose of this letter is to follow up on our (phone) conversation of (date) and satisfactorily resolve any outstanding issue(s) regarding the above-referenced account.

The problem(s) and/or outstanding issue(s) is (are) as follows:

✓ (List a problem)
✓ (List a problem)

(Explain the type of corrective action that should be taken and the reason for it [them] in a few sentences).

Please take the necessary action to correct the problem(s) outlined above and let me know, within a reasonable time frame, what action(s) you have decided to take.

Sincerely,

(FIRST NAME MI LAST NAME)
(Street address)
(City), (State) (Zip code)
(Phone # - where you can be contacted) - not required

Sample Letter to Credit Bureau

(City), (Date)

(Name of credit bureau)
(Street or P.O. address of credit bureau)
(City), (State) (Zip code)

Re: (Account #) - (Last Name, First Name, Middle Initial of person on credit report)

Dear (Title or name of contact person – or, if not known, To Whom It May Concern):

The purpose of this letter is to follow up on our (phone) conversation of (date) and satisfactorily resolve any outstanding issue(s) regarding the above-referenced credit report.

The problem(s) and/or outstanding issue(s) is (are) as follows:

- ✓ (List a problem)
- ✓ (List a problem)

(Explain the type of corrective action that should be taken and the reason for it [them] in a few sentences).

Please take the necessary action to correct the problem(s) outlined above and let me know, within a reasonable time frame, what action(s) you have decided to take.

Sincerely,

(FIRST NAME MI LAST NAME)
(Street address)
(City), (State) (Zip code)
(Phone # - where you can be contacted) - not required

Sample Letter to Miscellaneous Business

(City), (Date)

(Name of business)
(Street or P.O. address of business)
(City), (State) (Zip code)

Re: (Account #) - (Last Name, First Name, Middle Initial of person on account or conducting business)

Dear (Title or name of contact person – or, if not known, To Whom It May Concern):

The purpose of this letter is to follow up on our [phone] conversation of [date] and) satisfactorily resolve any outstanding issue(s) regarding my recent purchase of (indicate what item you bought).

The problem(s) and/or outstanding issue(s) is (are) as follows:

✓   (List a problem)
✓   (List a problem)

(Explain the type of corrective action that should be taken and the reason for it [them] in a few sentences).

Please take the necessary action to correct the problem(s) outlined above and let me know, within a reasonable time frame, what action(s) you have decided to take.

Sincerely,

(FIRST NAME MI LAST NAME)
(Street address)
(City), (State) (Zip code)
(Phone # - where you can be contacted) - not required

• Third Party Involvement.
Taking Administrative or Legal Action.

Okay, time has passed and either the business did not respond to your letter, or the response was unsatisfactory. If in your letter, you advised the business that administrative or legal action may, or would follow, now is the time to get a third party involved to help you resolve your problem.

If you choose to take **administrative action**, gather the copies of letters you sent and verification of receipt of the certified letter (if any) and sit down and prepare another letter.

You must first determine who to escalate this matter to. There appears to be a governmental agency and/or a corporate office that has oversight responsibility for just about anything that one encounters in life. But, how do you find out who that might be? You have several options:

- **The corporate headquarter**s Contact the business you're dealing with to find out the mailing address of their headquarters (if there is one).
- **Your local phone boo**k (White pages – government section – city, county, state, or federal) I recommend you stay as "local" as possible. Try to identify the responsible entity by subject matter (in this example, Contract Licensing, or the Consumer Protection Agency may be appropriate).
- **Your friends** and (other) neighbors that may have had similar experiences can help direct you.
- **Your local government** official or representatives (See Appendix A or B).
- **The local Chamber of Commerc**e
- **The local chapter of the Better Business Burea**u
- **Your attorney**

Once you have identified the "responsible" administrative oversight entity <u>it may save you time to call them first and verify that they do, in fact, have oversight jurisdiction</u>.

If there is more than one responsible entity, write down their mailing addresses for possible later use. Now you're ready to write a letter to take administrative follow-up action!
- Use a date and an address line.
- Re: Your account or claim # - followed by Last Name, First Name, MI of person on account or claim.
- In the first paragraph introduce yourself and the purpose of this letter (i.e. to seek their help in resolving a problem).
- Introduce the problem by way of a short synopsis and tell how that problem involves the business.
- Indicate what actions you took to resolve this problem and what the response was (include a copy of your original, follow-up letter(s) and any response you received and refer to them at this time).
- Request the entity to take appropriate action to resolve this problem.
- Indicate what action you intend to take should the problem not be resolved in a reasonable time frame.
- If you suspect that legal action may be taken by you at some point in time, your last paragraph should read: '*This letter has been sent by certified mail to ascertain legal receipt of same.*'
- Make sure to list any enclosures that you refer to in your letter, below your signature block.
- End the letter with 'Sincerely,' or some other appropriate courtesy, type your signature block and a way for you to be contacted (i.e. phone number or e-mail address and/or regular address to which mail can be sent).
- Below your signature block, list the name and address of any third party you are sending a copy of this letter to.
- Mail your letter as soon as practicable with sufficient postage – regular or certified – as appropriate, to all addresses. Keep a copy of this letter, together with all related correspondence in a Suspense file for further action, if any.

NOTE: Your letter should be informative, but not lengthy; organized, but not impersonal; respectful in content and language, but not timid. And, please, make use of "spell-check" or a dictionary!

HELP: Please see Sample Letter of Administrative Action on page 40.

Sample Letter of Administrative Action

(City, Date)

(Name of third party)
(Street or P. O. address)
(City), (State) (Zip code)

Re: (Business name) – (Your Last Name, First Name, Middle Initial of person on account, your account number)

Dear (Title and name of third party person – or 'To Whom It May Concern): **NOTE:** *It's best to obtain a contact person's name, if at all possible.*

My name is .... and the purpose of this letter is to seek your help in resolving a problem I am having with the above-referenced business.

(In a few sentences state the problem, your action, and the final decision the business made.

e.g. *My health care provider has denied my legitimate claims for reimbursement – See Attachment #1. In my response to the initial denial, I followed the appeals process and stated reasons why my original claim should be honored – See Attachment #2. My health care provider denied my appeal – See Attachment #3.*

Indicate why you think the final decision should have been decided in your favor.

e.g. *As stated previously to my health care provider, my illness was such that I had to avail myself of immediate emergency medical attention at a hospital that is not part of my provider's health care system. I was unable to communicate with the ambulance transport professionals prior to being transported, however, I did notify my health care provider, by phone, of my situation as soon as I was physically able to do so.*

I respectfully request that your agency assist me in having my health care provider take another look at my claim and because of my peculiar circumstances, they honor my original claim for reimbursement within a reasonable period of time – no longer than 30 days from date of this letter.)

I reserve the right to escalate this matter should it not be resolved within the above-mentioned time frame.

Respectfully yours,

(FIRST NAME MI LAST NAME)
(Street address)
(City), (State) (Zip code)
(Phone # - where you can be contacted) - not required.

cc: (Name and address of business you are having problems with)

NOTE: *Do not send any attachments – only a copy of this letter and send a copy of the <u>letter only if you think making the business aware of your action may result in favorable action.</u>*

If you choose to take **legal** action, gather all your notes and correspondence and **contact your attorney for further action** (*your copies of the notes and correspondence should help the attorney and you focus on what action to take – so take them with you for your initial appointment*).

If you choose to take the Small Claims Court route without the advice of an attorney, gather all your notes and correspondence, go to your local Small Claims Court and proceed to file a claim (*your copies of the notes and correspondence should help you fill out your claim – so take them with you when you file your claim*).

Don't forget to include in the compensation amount you desire: court costs (including amount to have papers served), if any, lost wages or vacation time, if any, and any other legitimate cost you incur as a result of this suit.

Follow any court instructions or lawyer advice you receive.

Make a note of the court date when you receive it and be there on time (with all pertinent documents) ready to present your case.

Once the proceedings are completed and the judge has ruled on your case, follow his/her instructions and keep all pertinent documents until final resolution and at least six months thereafter, unless otherwise instructed by the court.

HELP: **Please see Sample Letter of Legal Action on page 42.**

Sample Letter of Legal Action

(City, Date)

(Name of business)
(Street or P. O. address)
(City), (State) (Zip code)

Re: (Account number - Your Last Name, First Name, Middle Initial)

Dear (Name of business contact to whose last communication you are responding to):

The purpose of this letter is to advise you, pursuant to my earlier communication with you (copy attached) and in response to your latest communication, dated , that I am taking the following legal action against you and/or your business entity from (*indicate here Small Claims Court, or what ever judicial entity you are seeking legal relief from*).

(If you have an attorney): My legal representative will be contacting you shortly about this matter and you are to communicate with that representative only. (*List the attorney's name and address*).

Sincerely,

(FIRST NAME MI LAST NAME)
(Street address)
(City), (State) (Zip code)

◆ Follow up/Appeals Actions

Should your request for action be denied by a third party, the written denial almost always includes instructions on how to appeal. Follow the instructions carefully. If you have any questions, be sure to call the entity whose decision you are appealing. Then proceed as instructed.

Should the denial of your request either not provide for an appeal, or not address appeals, find out what the next supervisory level of the entity that denied your appeal is. If you don't know, call them and find out – including name of office supervisor, phone number, and mailing address.

Now you're ready to take follow-up and/or appeals action!

- Use a date and an address line.
- In the Re: line, place your Case #, LAST NAME, First & MI
- In the first paragraph introduce yourself and the purpose of the letter (i.e. to seek their help in appealing a written denial).
- End the letter with 'Sincerely,' or some other appropriate courtesy, type your signature block and a way for you to be contacted (i.e. phone number or e-mail address and/or regular address to which mail can be sent).
- Mail your letter as soon as practicable with sufficient postage – regular, or certified – as appropriate.
- Keep a copy of this letter, together with all related correspondence in a Suspense file for further action, if any.

NOTE: **Your letter should be informative, but not lengthy; organized, but not impersonal; respectful in content and language, but not timid. And, please, make use of "spell-check" or a dictionary!**

HELP: **Please see Sample Letter of Appeals Letter on page 44.**

Sample Letter of Appeals

(City, Date)

(Name of third party entity)
(Street or P. O. address)
(City), (State) (Zip code)

Re: (Case number - Your Last Name, First Name, Middle Initial)

Dear (Name of contact to whose last communication you are responding to):

Please be advised that I am appealing your decision in the aforementioned case, pursuant to the instructions you have furnished me.

The appeal is being forwarded under separate cover.

NOTE: (*If you are using the services of an attorney – please check with him/her first to see if this letter is warranted or necessary and follow his/her instructions*).

Sincerely,

(FIRST NAME MI LAST NAME)
(Street address)
(City), (State) (Zip code)

COMMUNICATING WITH GOVERNMENTAL AGENCIES

THERE MAY COME a time when you have to resolve a problem or an issue with a **governmental agency**. The **methods of communication** and the **content of** that **communicatio**n with a governmental agency, as well as any **third party involvement and/or follow-up/appeal** actions, are distinctly different, primarily in style, from communicating with a private party or a business.

◆ Methods of Communication.

Let's say you have a problem or an issue with a governmental agency. You can choose to address that problem or discuss that issue by:

Calling or visiting the agency in person. Regardless of the nature of your problem, always be respectful or at least civil to the person at the agency. Introduce yourself, if you don't already know each other, and inform him/her of your concern. Offer a reasonable solution, including your part, if any, in contributing to the resolution of that problem.

Example: *You have applied for Social Security benefits and you have received a response that your supporting documents are not in order. For your application to be considered certain corrections must first be made or certain additional documents must be presented. You notice that some of the information you provided when you first applied at your local Social Security office is incorrect, or insufficient. Present the facts, as you know them, and ask the person behind the counter to kindly assist you in resolving your concerns/problems. Listen to the official's response. Thank him/her for listening.*

If the response was positive: Go home, write down who you talked to, what was discussed and agreed upon and proceed to follow through. Keep the record of your discussion until the problem is resolved – your application has been approved.

If the response was negative, non-cooperative, or hostile: Ask for the name & address of that official and his or her supervisor. Go home, write down what was discussed, what you offered to help resolve the problem and the subordinate official's response. In the example you have several options, including *writing an official letter to the agency*, and/or *taking administrative or legal actions*.

Writing a letter to a governmental agency.

You have attempted to settle the matter in an informal way, and, for whatever reason, you did not accomplish your goal. It is time to put things "in writing."

Putting things "in writing," affords you the opportunity to accomplish several things:
- Create a written record of your attempts to settle a problem
- Organize things in a way that makes any future actions easier, and
- Serve as a point of reference for solving future problems.

You can literally use the **power in your pe**n by the use of handwriting, a typewriter, or – my preferred and recommended use – the handy-dandy computer.

♦ Contents of Communication

Whatever you decide to use to write your letter, make sure you keep these principles of good letter-writing in mind:

- Use a date and an address line.
- Use the **reference/case/account numbe**r you were assigned below the address in the subject-line as well as your name.
- In the first paragraph introduce yourself and indicate that this letter is a follow-up to a previous meeting/visit.
- (Re)introduce the problem and tell how that problem involves the addressee.
- (Re)offer a solution to that problem, your part in the solution, and how that solution would benefit you and the agency – as applicable.
- Request a reasonable timeline (usually 30 days – unless less time is more appropriate) by which you can expect a response from the addressee and state, in general, the possible consequences for not receiving a response in time, or receiving a negative response.
- If you suspect that legal action may be taken by you at some point in time, your last paragraph should read: *'This letter has been sent by certified mail to ascertain legal receipt of same.'*
- End the letter with 'Sincerely,' or some other appropriate courtesy, type your signature block and a way for you to be contacted (i.e. phone number or e-mail address and/or regular address to which mail can be sent).
- Mail your letter as soon as practicable with sufficient postage – regular, or certified – as appropriate.
- Keep a copy in a Suspense file for further action, if any.

NOTE: Your letter should be informative, but not lengthy; organized, but not impersonal; respectful in content and language, but not timid. And, please, make use of "spell-check" or a dictionary!

HELP: Please see Sample Letters (Local, State & Federal Offices, Legislative Branch, and Judicial Branch) as follows:

Sample Letter to Local Executive

(City), (State), (Date)

Mr. John Doe – Chief of Police (County Sheriff, etc.)
3456 Badge Drive, Ste. 100
(City), (State) (Zip code)

Dear Chief (Sheriff) Doe:

The purpose of this letter is to bring to your attention a situation that requires your investigation and corrective action.

For the past six weeks, my neighbors and I (along with my family members) have observed what appear to be drug dealings and acts of prostitution in our neighborhood, between the hours of 9:00 p.m. and 1:00 a.m., along with the resulting excessive traffic, idling cars, blaring car radios, loud cursing and arguing, as well as a few fights and many times, discarded (dirty) needles and prophylactics – indicating illicit sexual activities.

Ours is a family neighborhood and, as you can readily see, the activities outlined above constitute a breach of peace, a violation of law, and a danger to our children.

I would like to invite you – or your representative - to a neighborhood meeting at the above residence on (date), where we can discuss this matter further and perhaps have you commit to a plan of action. Please call me at (leave phone number) prior to that date to confirm your attendance, or to see if another date might be more suitable to your busy schedule. (Please expect approximately 40 people in attendance).

Sincerely,

(CAPITALIZE YOUR NAME: First, Middle Init, Last)
(Street address, Apt. or Ste. #)
(City), (State) (Zip code)

Sample Letter to Local Legislator

(City), (State), (Date)

Hon. John Doe – City Councilmember
(Address of City Hall)
(City), (State) (Zip code)

Dear Council(wo)man (Last Name):

The purpose of this letter is to bring to your attention a situation that requires your investigation and corrective action.

For the past six weeks, my neighbors and I (along with my family members) have observed what appear to be drug dealings and acts of prostitution in our neighborhood, between the hours of 9:00 p.m. and 1:00 a.m., along with the resulting excessive traffic, idling cars, blaring car radios, loud cursing and arguing, as well as a few fights and many times, discarded (dirty) needles and prophylactics – indicating illicit sexual activities.

Ours is a family neighborhood and, as you can readily see, the activities outlined above constitute a breach of peace, a violation of law, and a danger to our children.

I would like to invite you – or your representative – to a neighborhood meeting at the above residence on (date), where we can discuss this matter further and perhaps have you come up with a plan of action to eliminate this nuisance. Please call me at (leave phone number) prior to that date to confirm your attendance – or to see if another date might be more suitable to your busy schedule. (Please expect approximately 40 people in attendance). You are welcome to bring with you any subject matter expert guest you choose.

Sincerely,

(CAPITALIZE YOUR NAME: First, Middle Init, Last)
(Street address, Apt. or Ste. #)
(City), (State) (Zip code)

Sample Letter to Local Judiciary

(City), (State), (Date)

Hon. John Doe – Municipal Court Judge
(Address of City Hall)
(City), (State) (Zip Code)
Re: Case # (LAST, First & MI)

Dear Judge (Last Name):

Please be advised that the document your Honor requested (list name of document, form number, etc.) is attached.

Respectfully,

(CAPITALIZE YOUR NAME: First, Middle Init, Last)
(Street address, Apt. or Ste. #)
(City), (State) (Zip code)

Enclosure

[**NOTE:** *It might be helpful, before sending a letter to any member of the judiciary, to ascertain from the judge's staff if such a letter (from a non-lawyer) is appropriate, and if it is, what the content requirements might be. Also, it might be helpful to seek out the advice of a competent attorney before you mail anything to any court.*]

Sample Letter to State Executive

(City), (State), (Date)

Mr. John Doe – Chief of State Police (Highway Patrol, etc.)
3456 Badge Drive, Ste 100
(City), (State) (Zip code)

Dear Chief Doe:

The purpose of this letter is to bring to your attention a situation that requires a fair solution, and to request your assistance in obtaining it.

On Saturday, (date) at 7:30 p.m., I was traveling on Interstate 5, near Sacramento, California, when I was pulled over by one of your officers (badge #) and cited for using the diamond lane while being a single occupant in my car. I was not cited for any other infraction of the law.

I tried to explain to the officer that the signs posted indicated that the diamond lanes are operational only Mon. -Fri. (6:00 a.m. – 10:00 a.m. and 3:00p.m. – 7:00 p.m.) The officer was rude and would not allow me to say anything at all! He just issued the ticket with the time and date of the "violation" indicated (copy of citation is attached) and handed it to me.

I will, of course, take the time and effort to fight this in court. If the officer had listened to me (or had been aware of the obvious – the sign I was referring to), I would not have to be inconvenienced with a court appearance.

Please educate your officers as to the diamond-lane signs posted in certain localities and emphasize the need for them to be courteous and professional when dealing with members of the public they profess to "serve."

Sincerely,

(CAPITALIZE YOUR NAME: First, Middle Init, Last)
(Street address, Apt. or Ste. #)
(City), (State) (Zip code)

Enclosure

Sample Letter to State Legislator

(City), (State), (Date)

Honorable John Doe – (Assembly Member, Senator)
The State Capitol
(City), (State) (Zip Code)

Dear (Assembly Member, Senator) Doe:

The purpose of this letter is to bring to your attention a situation that requires a fair solution, and to request your assistance in obtaining it.

I am a 65-year-old widow, who for the past several years has depended on my monthly State Disability check to live on.

On (date) I received a notice from the State Disability office (copy attached) that my monthly payment will be cut by 25% because of a clerical error previously made – which had the effect of overpaying me for the total of $2,500.00 - until that amount is recouped.

This 25% cut will be devastating to my livelihood and will mean that I may have to choose (some months) between buying food or medicine.

I respectfully request your intervention on my behalf with the State Disability office to encourage them to either waive their reimbursement requirement, since the error was theirs, or, if that cannot be reasonably done, to have them reduce my monthly reimbursement to a more reasonable amount, perhaps over a longer period of time.

Thank you for your time and effort in this matter, and I hope to hear from you soon.

Sincerely,

(CAPITALIZE YOUR NAME: First, Middle Init, Last)
(Street address, Apt. or Ste. #)
(City), (State) (Zip code)

Enclosure

Sample Letter to State Judiciary

(City), (State), (Date)

Hon. John Doe – Superior Court Judge (*or address it to: Clerk of the Superior Court or whatever the name of the State Court is in your jurisdiction*)
(Address of City Hall)
(City), (State) (Zip code)

Re: Case # (LAST, First & MI)

Dear Judge (or Clerk of the Court) (Last Name):

Please be advised that the document your Honor (the judge) requested (list name of document, form number, etc.) is attached.

Respectfully,

(CAPITALIZE YOUR NAME: First, Middle Init, Last)
(Street address, Apt. or Ste. #)
(City), (State) (Zip code)

Enclosure

[**NOTE:** *It might be helpful, before sending a letter to any member of the judiciary, to ascertain from the judge's staff (clerk's office) if such a letter (from a non-lawyer) is appropriate, and if it is, what the content requirements might be. Also, it might be helpful to seek out the advice of a competent attorney before you mail anything to any court.*]

Sample Letter to Federal Executive

(City), (State), (Date)

Mr. John Doe – (Title & Department/Office)
(Address) (Suite)
(City), (State) (Zip code)

Dear Mr. (Ms). (or Title) Doe:

The purpose of this letter is to bring to your attention a situation that requires a fair solution and to request your assistance in obtaining it.

(Briefly describe your situation/problem in a few sentences).

(Briefly describe what action(s) you took to resolve the matter and mention any attachment you may want to include – list below your signature block).

I would appreciate if you would look into this matter, or appoint someone else to do it, as appropriate and respond to me as soon as you possibly can.

Thank you for your time and effort. I hope to hear from you or your representative soon.

Sincerely,

(CAPITALIZE YOUR NAME: First, Middle Init, Last)
(Street address, Apt. or Ste. #)
(City), (State) (Zip code)

Enclosure

Sample Letter to Federal Legislator

(City), (State), (Date)

Honorable John Doe – (US Representative, US Senator)
The Capitol
Washington, D.C. 20515

Dear (Congressman/woman, Senator) Doe:

The purpose of this letter is to bring to your attention a situation that requires a fair solution and to request your assistance in obtaining it.

I am a 65-year-old widow, who for the past several years has depended on my monthly Social Security check to live on.

On Apr 1, 2007, I moved to a new address. I notified the Social Security office of my move (copy of notice attached). However, I have not yet received my monthly check.

I'm becoming somewhat desperate. My family has been helping me financially, but it is becoming a hardship for them as well. I am unable to get anyone at Social Security to assist me in any meaningful way.

I am a registered voter, have been for most of my life, and I am asking you to assist me in getting my Social Security checks restored and properly delivered.

Thank for your time and effort in this matter. I hope to hear from you soon.

Sincerely,

(CAPITALIZE YOUR NAME: First, Middle Init, Last)
(Street address, Apt. or Ste. #)
(City), (State) (Zip code)

Enclosure

Sample Letter to Federal Judiciary

(City), (State), (Date)

Hon. John Doe – US District Court Judge – (Specify District) (*or address it to: Clerk of the US District Court or whatever the name of the US District Court is in your jurisdiction*)
(Address)
(City), (State) (Zip code)

Re: Case # (LAST, First & MI)

Dear Judge (or Clerk of the Court) (Last Name):

Please be advised that the document your Honor (the judge) requested (list name of document, form number, etc. is attached.

Respectfully,

(CAPITALIZE YOUR NAME: First, Middle Init, Last)
(Street address, Apt. or Ste. #)
(City), (State) (Zip code)

Enclosure

[**NOTE:** *It might be helpful, before sending a letter to any member of the judiciary, to ascertain from the judge's staff (clerk's office) if such a letter (from a non-lawyer) is appropriate, and if it is, what the content requirements might be. Also, it might be helpful to seek out the advice of a competent attorney before you mail anything to any court.*]

◆ Third Party Involvement
Taking Administrative or Legal Actions

Okay, time has passed and the governmental agency did not respond to your letter, or the response was negative. If in your letter, you advised that administrative or legal action may, or would follow, now is the time to get a third party involved to help you resolve your problem.

If you choose to take **administrative action**, gather the copies of letter(s) you sent and verification of receipt of the certified letter, if any, and sit down and prepare another letter.

You must first determine who to escalate this matter to. You know the old adage: *Everyone has a boss.* This is especially true for governmental agencies. But, how do you find out who that might be? You have several options:

- **Your Compute**r - Go on line and do your research by simply using keywords, then follow through for contact information. See **Communication Resources for Citizens, Clients and/or Consumers on page 63.**
- **Your local phone boo**k (White pages – governmental section – city, county, state, or federal). I recommend you stay as "local" as possible. Try to identify the responsible entity by subject matter (in this example, the Regional Social Security office may be appropriate).
- **Your friend**s and other family members or neighbors may have had similar experiences and can help direct you.
- **Call the local agenc**y you were dealing with and find out their supervising department and the address.
- **Your legislative** representative's office. See Appendix B.
- **Your attorney**.

Once you have identified the "responsible" entity it may save you time to call them first and verify that they do, in fact, have oversight jurisdiction.
If there is more than one responsible entity, write down their mailing addresses for possible later use.
Now you're ready to take administrative action!
- Use a date and an address line.
- Use the **reference/case/account numbe**r you were assigned below the address line as well as your name
- In the first paragraph introduce yourself and the purpose of this letter (i.e. to seek their help in resolving a problem).
- Introduce the problem by way of a short synopsis and tell how that problem involves that agency.
- Indicate what actions you took to resolve this problem and what the response was. Include a copy of your original, follow-up letter(s) and any response you received, and refer to them at this time.
- Request the entity to take appropriate action to resolve this problem in a timely manner.
- Indicate what action you intend to take should the problem not be resolved in a reasonable time frame.
- If you suspect that legal action may be taken by you at some point in time, your last paragraph should read: *'This letter has been sent by certified mail to ascertain legal receipt of same.'*
- End the letter with 'Sincerely,' or some other appropriate courtesy, type your signature block and a way for you to be contacted (i.e. phone number or e-mail address and/or regular address to which mail can be sent).
- Mail your letter as soon as practicable with sufficient postage – regular, or certified – as appropriate, to all addresses.
- Keep a copy of this letter, together with all related correspondence in a Suspense file for further action, if any.

NOTE: Your letter should be informative, but not lengthy; organized, but not impersonal; respectful in content and language, but not timid. And, please, make use of "spell-check" or a dictionary!

HELP: Please see Sample Letter of Administrative Action on page 59.

Sample Letter of Administrative Action – Governmental Entity

(City, Date)

(Name of governmental entity you are seeking help from)
(Street or P. O. address)
(City), (State) (Zip code)

Re: (Name of governmental entity you are appealing from) – (Your Last Name, First Name, Middle Initial of person on account, your account number)

Dear (Title and name of contact person – or: To Whom It May Concern): **NOTE**: *It's best to obtain a contact person's name, if at all possible.*

My name is   and the purpose of this letter is to seek your help in resolving a problem I am having with the above-referenced entity/department.

(In a few sentences state the problem, your action, any additional mitigating information you may have, and the final decision the governmental entity made).

(Indicate why you think the final decision should have been decided in your favor).

I respectfully request that your agency assist me in having (the aforementioned entity/department) reconsider their original decision, based on the additional information I provided you, and come to a satisfactory conclusion.

Respectfully yours,

(FIRST NAME MI LAST NAME)
(Street address)
(City), (State) (Zip code)
(Phone # - where you can be contacted) - not required.

cc: (Name & address, including the name of the person you have been dealing with, of the governmental entity you are having problems with)

NOTE: *Do not send any attachments – only a copy of this letter and send a copy of the <u>letter only if you think making the business aware of your action may result in favorable action</u>.*

> If you choose to take **legal** action, gather all your notes and correspondence and **contact your attorney for further action.** *Your copies of the notes and correspondence should help the attorney and you focus on what action to take – so take them with you for your initial appointment.*

HELP: **Please see Sample Letter of Legal Action on page 60.**

Sample Letter of Legal Action – Governmental Entity

(City, Date)

(Name of governmental entity you are taking legal action against)
(Street or P. O. address)
(City), (State), (Zip code)

Re: (Case number - Your Last Name, First Name, Middle Initial)

Dear (Name of governmental contact to whose last communication you are responding):

The purpose of this letter is to advise you, pursuant to my earlier communication with you (copy attached) and in response to your latest communication, dated , that I am taking the following legal action against (name of entity/department): (*Indicate here what legal action you are taking, and the court you are seeking relief from*).

Sincerely,

(FIRST NAME MI LAST NAME)
(Street address)
(City), (State) (Zip code)

NOTE: *If you have an attorney – seek advice first. If your attorney wants you to send this letter: My legal representative will be contacting you shortly about this matter and you are to communicate with that representative only. (List the attorney's name and address). If you don't have an attorney, I advise you to seek legal counsel before taking any legal action.*

◆ Follow up/Appeal Actions

Should your request for action be denied by a governmental entity or a third party, the written denial almost always includes instructions on how to appeal. Follow the instructions to the letter. If you have any questions, be sure to call the entity whose decision you are appealing. Then proceed as instructed.

Should the denial of your request either not provide for an appeal, or not address appeals, find out what the next supervisory level of the entity that denied your appeal is. If you don't know, call them and find out – including name of office supervisor, phone number, and mailing address.

Now you're ready to take follow-up and/or appeal action!

- Use a date and an address line.
- Use the **reference/case/account numbe**r you were assigned below the address line, as well as your name.
- In the first paragraph introduce yourself and the purpose of this letter (i.e. to seek their help in appealing a written denial).
- Introduce the problem by way of a short synopsis and tell how that problem involves that agency.
- Indicate what actions you took to resolve this problem and what the response was. Include a copy of your original, follow-up letter(s), copies of documents originally submitted, and any response you received and refer to them at this time.
- Request the entity to take appropriate action to reverse the original decision.
- If you suspect that legal action may be taken by you at some point in time, your last paragraph should read: *'This letter has been sent by certified mail to ascertain legal receipt of same.'*
- End the letter with 'Sincerely,' or some other appropriate courtesy, type your signature block and a way for you to be contacted (i.e. phone number or e-mail address and/or regular address to which mail can be sent).
- Send a copy of this appeal to the entity whose denial you are appealing, unless the appeal directions tell you otherwise.
- Mail your letter as soon as practicable with sufficient postage – regular or certified – as appropriate, to all involved addresses.
- Keep a copy of this letter, together with all related correspondence in a Suspense file for further action, if any.

NOTE: **Your letter should be informative, but not lengthy; organized, but not impersonal; respectful in content and language, but not timid. And, please, make use of "spell-check" or a dictionary!**

HELP: **Please see Sample Appeal Letter on page 62.**

Sample Letter of Appeal – Governmental Entity

(City, Date)

(Name of governmental entity/department/agency)
(Street or P. O. address)
(City), (State) (Zip code)

Re: (Case number - Your Last Name, First Name, Middle Initial)

Dear (Name of contact to whose last communication you are responding to):

Please be advised that I am appealing your decision in the aforementioned case, pursuant to the instructions you have furnished me.

The appeal is being forwarded under separate cover.

(NOTE: *If you are using the services of an attorney – please check with him/her first to see if this letter is warranted or necessary and follow his/her instructions).*

Sincerely,

(FIRST NAME, MI, LAST NAME)
(Street address)
(City), (State) (Zip code)

III

COMMUNICATION RESOURCES FOR CITIZENS, CLIENTS AND/OR CONSUMERS

IN TODAY'S WORLD there are many tools available. They are literally at your fingertips, if and when you decide to communicate:

✓ As a Citizen

Since, as previously stated, your right to communicate with just about anyone in government, is constitutionally protected, there are many ways to find out contact information.

(1) **Use your Computer** – Get on line and key in the jurisdiction you want (i.e. federal, state, or local). Social Security, the Internal Revenue Service Center and/or the US Veteran's Administration are federal agencies or departments. Key in the department, then look at their home page for contact information. Similarly, Social Welfare, state taxes, and or the State Veteran's Administration are state agencies. Key in the department (preceded by the state's name) and, again, look at their home page for contact information. For county or city contacts use the same methods described here.

(2) **Use your Phone Book** – the section that usually precedes the White Pages – to find contact information; either the mailing address and, if not available, the phone number. Then call to get the mailing address. The government section is usually divided into city, county, state, and federal sections.

(3) **Use your Local Library** – Ask to use the computer, then follow (1) above. If no computers are available, or you are not computer literate, kindly ask the librarian for assistance, so you can find out the governmental contact information you need. Bring a pencil and paper, jot down the information, or check out the material. Then go home and go to work!

✓ As a Client

There may come a time when seeking legal advice is not only necessary, but certainly the smart thing to do. Here are several ways to go about doing just that:

(1) **Use your Computer** – Get on line and key in the words: Legal Assistance. Sit back and check out the various avenues available to you. Some legal assistance organizations offer free help (usually they require that you meet a certain criteria), or they offer legal referral. In any case, you should be able to find contact information – then 'go shopping either on line or by phone,' to get the information you're seeking.

(2)   **Use your Phone Book** – usually the Yellow Pages – for listings of Legal Assistance or Legal Clinics. Jot down the phone numbers of at least three, then call and see what they have to offer, and what their fees are.

(3)   **Use your Local Library** - Ask to use the computer, then follow (1) above. If no computers are available, or you are not computer literate, kindly ask the librarian for assistance, so you can find out the Legal Assistance or Legal Clinic contact information you need. Bring a pencil and paper, jot down the information or check out the material. Then go home do what I recommend in (2) above.

✓ As a Consumer

If you need contact information for a particular business, be it local, regional, or national, again, using your computer, your phone book, or the local library maybe your best way to go.

(1)   **Use your Computer** – Get on line and key in the name of the business you're seeking contact information for. Most businesses probably have a home page on the World Wide Web. Just look for "Contact," or "Customer Service" and click on that link. This is also a good way to find out who that particular business' boss is (e.g. You're having problems with a chainstore business. You can get the local store manager's contact information and/or the regional, or even national contact information to address your issues to, when and if necessary. If the business is not listed, or is a private business ["mom and pop" store] search for the local county, city, or state Chamber of Commerce contact information, or search for the Better Business Bureau in your jurisdiction).

(2)   **Use your Phone Book** - usually the White Pages, or the Yellow Pages. By using the name of the business you can usually find out the address and/or the phone number. Call them and get the contact information you need.

(3)   **Use your Local Library** - Ask to use the computer, then follow (1) above. If no computers are available, or you are not computer literate, kindly ask the librarian for assistance, so you can find out the business contact information you need. Bring a pencil and paper, jot down the information or check out the material. Then go home do what I recommend in (2) above.

Of course there are other ways to find out contact information or to point you in the right direction, by asking family members, friends, and/or co-workers.

IV

APPENDIX A

FEDERAL (EXECUTIVE) AGENCIES and Commissions*

A

AMTRAK
www.amtrak.com
Appalachian Regional Commission
www.arc.gov
Architectural and Transportation Barriers Compliance Board
www.access-board.gov

B

Bureau of Alcohol, Tobacco, & Firearms
www.atf.treas.gov
Bureau of Labor Statistics
www.bls.gov
Bureau of the Census
www.census.gov
Bureau of Transportation Statistics
www.bts.gov

C

Centers for Medicare and Medicaid Services
cms.hhs.gov
Commission on Civil Rights
www.usccr.gov
Consumer Product Safety Commission (CPSC)
www.cpsc.gov

D

Drug Enforcement Administration
www.usdoj.gov/dea

E

Environmental Protection Agency (EPA)
www.epa.gov
Equal Employment Opportunity Commission
www.eeoc.gov

F

Farm Credit Administration (FCA)
www.fca.gov
Federal Accounting Standards Advisory Board
www.fasab.gov
Federal Aviation Administration
www.faa.gov
Federal Bureau of Investigation
www.fbi.gov
Federal Communications Commission (FCC)
www.fcc.gov
Federal Deposit Insurance Corporation (FDIC)
www.fdic.gov
Federal Election Commission (FEC)
www.fec.gov
Federal Emergency Management Agency (FEMA)
www.fema.gov
Federal Energy Regulatory Commission
www.ferc.gov
Federal Highway Administration
www.fhwa.dot.gov
Federal Housing Finance Board (FHFB)
www.fhfb.gov
Federal Labor Relations Authority
www.flra.gov
Federal Mediation & Conciliation Service
www.fmcs.gov
Federal Mine Safety & Health Review Commission
www.fmshrc.gov
Federal Railroad Administration
www.fra.dot.gov
Federal Reserve System
www.federalreserve.gov
Federal Retirement Thrift Investment Board
www.frtib.gov
Federal Trade Commission (FTC)
www.ftc.gov

Food & Drug Administration
www.fda.gov

G

General Services Administration (GSA)
www.gsa.gov
Ginnie Mae
www.ginniemae.gov
Government Accountability Office
www.gao.gov

I

Institute of Museum and Library Services
www.imls.gov
Inter-American Development Bank
www.iadb.org
Internal Revenue Services
www.irs.ustreas.gov
International Labor Organization
www.us.ilo.org
International Trade Commission (USITC)
www.usitc.gov

L

Legal Services Corporation
www.lsc.gov

M

Medicare Payment Advisory Commission
www.medpac.gov

N

National Council on Disability (NCD)
www.ncd.gov
National Credit Union Administration
www.ncua.gov
National Endowment for the Arts
http://arts.endow.gov
National Endowment for the Humanities
www.neh.gov
National Highway Traffic Safety Administration
www.nhtsa.dot.gov
National Institute of Justice

www.ojp.usdoj.gov/nij
National Institute of Mental Health
www.nimh.nih.gov
National Institutes of Health
www.nih.gov
National Labor Relations Board
www.nlrb.gov
National Mediation Board
www.nmb.gov
National Park Service
www.nps.gov
National Security Agency (NSA)
www.nsa.gov
National Telecommunications Information Administration
www.ntia.doc.gov
National Transportation Safety Board www.ntsb.gov

O

Occupational Safety and Health Review Commission
www.oshrc.gov
Office of Government Ethics
www.usoge.gov
Office of Personnel Management (OPM)
www.opm.gov

P

Patent & Trademark Office
www.uspto.gov
Peace Corps
www.peacecorps.gov
Pension Benefit Guaranty Corporation (PBGC)
www.pbgc.gov
Postal Rate Commission
www.prc.gov

R

Railroad Retirement Board (RRB)
www.rrb.gov

S

Securities Exchange Commission (SEC)
www.sec.gov
Selective Service System (SSS)
www.sss.gov
Small Business Administration (SBA)

www.sba.gov
Social Security Administration (SSA)
www.ssa.gov
Substance Abuse & Mental Health Services Administration
www.samhsa.gov
Surface Transportation Board
www.stb.dot.gov

T

Tennessee Valley Authority www.tva.gov
Trade and Development Agency
www.tda.gov

U

U.S. Citizenship and Immigration Services
www.uscis.gov/portal/site/uscis
U.S. Customs Service
www.customs.gov
U.S. Fish and Wildlife Service
www.fws.gov
U.S. Forest Service
www.fs.fed.us
U.S. Government Printing Office
www.gpo.gov
U.S. Marshals Service
www.usdoj.gov/marshals/
U.S. Office of Government Ethics (USOGE)
www.usoge.gov
U.S. Treasury www.treas.gov
United States Postal Service (USPS)
www.usps.gov

V

Voice of America (VOA)
www.voa.gov

W

Walter Reed Army Medical Center
www.wramc.amedd.army.mil

Appendix B – Additional Help and Resources

United States Congress
www.visi.com/juan/congress/ (Click on side panel for committees, commissions, etc.)

Federal Judicial Branch
www.uscourts.gov/ (Click on side panel for contact information.)